Each One Specially

By Carol Greene

Illustrated by Maritz Communications Company

CONCORDIA®

Publishing House
St. Louis

BOOK ONE of the NEW Concordia Sex Education Series

The titles in the series:

BOOK 1:   EACH ONE SPECIALLY
BOOK 2:   I WONDER WHY
BOOK 3:   HOW YOU GOT TO BE YOU
BOOK 4:   THE NEW YOU
BOOK 5:   LORD OF LIFE, LORD OF ME
BOOK 6:   SEXUALITY: GOD'S PRECIOUS GIFT
               TO PARENTS AND CHILDREN

Developed under the auspices of the Family Life Department
Board for Parish Services
The Lutheran Church—Missouri Synod

Copyright © 1982
Concordia Publishing House
3558 South Jefferson Avenue
Saint Louis, Missouri 63118

MANUFACTURED IN THE UNITED STATES OF AMERICA

Library of Congress Cataloging in Publication Data

Greene, Carol.
  Each one specially.

  (New Concordia sex education series; book 1)
  Summary: Sex instruction for the preschooler, presented from a Christian
point of view.
  1. Sex instruction for children. 2. Sex instruction for children—Religious
aspects—Christianity. [1. Sex instruction for children. 2. Sex—Religious
aspects—Christianity. 3. Christian life] I. Title. II. Series.
HQ53.G66 1982   241'.66   82-8104
ISBN 0-570-08475-X   AACR2

---

  3 4 5 6 7 8 9 10   PP   91 90 89 88 87 86 85

Editor's Foreword

This book is one of a series of six published under the auspices of the Board for Parish Services of The Lutheran Church—Missouri Synod through its Family Life Department.

Other books in the series are: *I Wonder Why* (ages 6—8); *How You Got to be You* (ages 8—11); *The New You* (ages 11—14); *Lord of Life, Lord of Me* (ages 14+); and *Sexuality: God's Precious Gift to Parents and Children.*

As the title suggests, the last book is designed for adults, to help them deal with their own sexuality, as well as provide practical assistance for married and single parents in their role as sex educators in the home.

Each One Specially is the first book in the series. It is written especially for children of preschool age—and, of course, for the parents, teachers, and other significant grownups who will read the book to the child. (See the "Note to Grownups" at the end of this book for suggestions on using the book and ways to communicate Christian values in sex education in the home.)

Like its predecessor, the New Concordia Sex Education Series provides information about the social-psychological and physiological aspects of human sexuality. But more: it does so from a distinctively Christian point of view, in the context of our relationship to the God who created us and redeemed us in Jesus Christ.

The series presents sex as another good gift from God which is to be used responsibly.

Each book in the series is graded—in vocabulary and in the amount of information it provides. It answers the questions which persons at each age level typically ask.

Because children vary widely in their growth rates and interest levels, parents and other concerned adults will want to preview each book in the series, directing the child to the next-graded book when he/she is ready for it.

In additon to reading each book, you can use them as starting points for casual conversation and when answering other questions a child might have.

This book can also be used as a mini-unit or as part of another course of study in a Christian school setting. (Correlated filmstrips are available for curricular use.) Whenever the book is used in a class setting, it's important to let the parents know beforehand, since they have the prime responsibility for the sex education of their children.

While parents will appreciate the help of the school, they will want to know what is being taught. As the Christian home and the Christian school work together, Christian values in sex education can be more effectively strengthened.

Frederick J. Hofmeister, M. D., FACOG, Wauwatosa, Wis., served as medical adviser for the series.

Rev. Ronald W. Brusius, secretary of family life education/Board for Parish Services, served as chief subject matter consultant.

In addition to the staffs of the Board for Parish Services and Concordia Publishing House, the following special consultants helped conceptualize the series: Darlene Armbruster, Betty Brusius, Margaret Gaulke, Priscilla Henkelman, Lee Hovel, Robert Miles, Margaret Noettl, and Rex Spicer.

Earl H. Gaulke

I am he.
God made me.

I am she.
God made me.

God made each one specially.
God made YOU too.
Didn't He do a good job?

I am not like you.

I like to hop.

I like yellow.

I like chocolate
ice cream cones.

I am not like you.
I am ME.
But I like you.

And I am not like you.

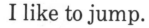

I like to jump.

I like red.

I like vanilla
ice cream cones.

I am not like you.
I am ME.
But I like you.

You are not like us.
You are YOU.
God made YOU that way.
But we like YOU.

God gave us eyes
to see with

and ears to hear with

and noses to smell with

and mouths
to taste and talk with.

He gave us hands and feet
and fingers and toes
and elbows and knees
and minds to think with.

God made each one of us
specially . . .

God gave girls
a vagina.
It is on the inside.
That is the best
place for it.

God gave us wonderful bodies.
He gave you one too.

God gave boys
a penis.
It is on the outside.
That is the best
place for it.

God gave us wonderful bodies.
He gave you one too.

You know, God made
a lot of shes,
and shes can do
a lot of things.

My mother
is a she.

So is my grandma
and my cousin

and that nurse

and that banker

TELLER

and that painter

and the person
driving that truck.

I'm glad
I'm a she.

God made a lot
of hes too,
and hes can do
a lot of things.

My father
is a he.

So is my
grandpa

and my uncle

and that lion tamer

and that cook

and that teacher

and the person
flying that plane.

I'm glad
I'm a he.

How did God make us?
I don't know. Let's ask.

God made you
in a special way.
You see . . .

Sometimes a grownup he
and a grownup she
love each other very much.
So, with God's blessing, they get married.
Then they decide
that they want
a little baby
to share their love.

God answers their prayer and then
the baby grows inside its mother
for nine months.
It is safe and warm.
Sometimes it wiggles and kicks.
When it gets bigger,
you can feel it from the outside.

I think that's great!

Me too.

After nine months
the baby is born.
It comes out through the mother's vagina.
The mother and father
are very glad to see it.

That is how God made YOU.
That is how He makes all people.

God does another great thing.
He puts people into families.
That's so they can
take care of each other
and love each other.

Some families are small.

Some families are big.

19

There are many different kinds of families.

What kind of family
did God put YOU into?

Families do things together.

I like to hug my mother.
She's a good hugger.

I like to play ball
with my brother . .

I like to listen
to my grandma
tell stories.

I'm glad God put me
into a family.

I like to feed my sister.

I like to go fishing with my grandpa.

I like to kiss my father. He feels scratchy, but I like it.

I'm glad God put me into a family.

What do YOU like to do with YOUR family?

God puts us into
a church family too.
People in church
families take care
of each other
and love each other.

Some church families are small.

Some church families are big.

There are many different kinds of church families.

What kind of church family did God put YOU into?

Church families do things together.

I like to make things in Sunday school.

I like to learn about Jesus.

I like to sing songs.

I'm glad God put me into a church family.

I like to see
my friends
at church.

I like
to look
at the
windows.

I like to pray
to Jesus.

I'm glad God
put me into a
church family.

**What do YOU like to do
with YOUR church family?**

I am he.
God loves me.

I am she.
God loves me.

God loves each one specially.
That is why He is so good to us.
God loves YOU too.
Aren't you glad He does?

Note to Grownups

When that first question about sex tumbles off a toddler's tongue, the consulted adult has often been pictured reacting in a number of less-than-desirable ways: with embarrassment ("Mumble, mumble, go ask your mother"); with evasion ("Mommy thinks she hears the telephone"); or perhaps with flights of fantasy ("Once there was a big white bird . . . "). Although these pictures are probably as false as any stereotype, the fact remains that many adults prefer to approach their children's questions with the aid of other resources. This book is designed to provide that aid and to do so in a Christian context. But no one book can anticipate the needs of all preschoolers and, when push comes to shove, adults must still rely heavily on their own sensitivity and common sense. A few pointers, however, might help.

Listen carefully to the question being asked and answer it precisely. If Jenny wants to know why Mrs. Blackwell's tummy is so fat, explain that Mrs. Blackwell is going to have a baby (if this is the case!). "But it isn't in her tummy. It's in a special place called the uterus that God made for babies before they are born." If Jenny follows this with another question, answer it with equal honesty and continue to do so until her curiosity is satisfied. Don't be surprised if she repeats the same series of questions tomorrow or three weeks from now. For a number of psychological reasons, the small child thrives on repetition. Be sure, though, that you are consistent in the answers you give.

It is always wise to use correct terminology with small children in such discussions, both to help them know that you are taking them quite seriously and to prevent later embarrassment.

Above all, remember that sexuality is far more than the reproductive organs with which each of us is born. It is a tremendous gift of God and colors almost everything we are and do. The sense of wonder and joy you feel in your own sexuality and that of your child is perhaps the most important thing you can teach him or her.

"Male and female He created them. . . . And God saw everything that He had made, and behold, it was very good" (Genesis 1:27, 31).